As of 6/7/05

MICHIGAN SNAKES

A Field Guide and Pocket Reference
by

J. Alan Holman
James H. Harding
Marvin M. Hensley
Glenn R. Dudderar

Created 2001
lost Vol, 2008
Use: 12

MSU Museum
MSU Department of Zoology
MSU Department of Fisheries and Wildlife

Second Edition (*Third Printing*), 1999

MSU is an Affirmative-Action/Equal-Opportunity Institution. Extension programs and materials are available to all without regard to race, color, national origin, sex, disability, age or religion. Issued in furtherance of Extension work in agriculture and home economics, acts of May 8 and June 30, 1914, in cooperation with the U.S. Department of Agriculture. Arlen Leholm, Extension Director, Michigan State University, E. Lansing, MI 48824.

Acknowledgements

Photography:
R. W. VanDevender
James Harding
William Leonard
Sharon Cummings

Editorial assistance:
Citizens Non-Game Advisory Committee
Technical Advisory Committee on Amphibians and Reptiles
Robert Hess, DNR
Game Wildlife Fund
Natural Heritage Pro

Reptiles (an animal group that includes the turtles, crocodilians, lizards and snakes) are fascinating to many people, and snakes, along with the dinosaurs, are perhaps the most fascinating of reptiles. Unlike the dinosaurs, snakes are still living today, so they can be observed, studied and enjoyed. Michigan has 18 species of snakes, only one of which is venomous, and it occurs only in the Lower Peninsula.

Like all living reptiles, snakes have backbones (an internal bony skeleton) and scaly skin. They breathe air, get their body warmth from their surroundings, and hibernate in winter if they live where the temperature goes below freezing for long periods. Snakes do not have legs, external ears or movable eyelids. They have a transparent, immovable eye covering; a dry, scaly outer skin that is shed in one piece; a single row of wide belly scales; and a skull with movable bones and loosely connected jaws that can spread widely so food can be swallowed whole.

This book is a reference for the identification of Michigan snakes, but other subjects—such as snake behavior, habitats, conservation and snakebite treatment—are included to help you better understand and appreciate snakes. This book is intended for the general public and is not a detailed work for the professional herpetologist. Consult the books on page 72 for additional information on snakes.

One easy way to identify a Michigan snake is to compare it with the pictures in this bulletin. If you find a picture that looks like the snake, then look at the range map to see if the species is known to occur in the area where you

2

observed or caught it. If not, your identification may be incorrect. If the picture and range agree with what your snake looks like and where you found it, then carefully read the "identification" section to confirm your identification. Note that the size range given for each species is the total length for mature (adult) individuals.

The "habitat and habits" section is also useful in snake identification. A thick-bodied snake with an upturned nose ("identification" section) found in a sandy area eating a toad ("habitat and habits" section) can positively be identified as an Eastern Hog-nosed Snake in Michigan, even without the aid of a picture.

If you can look at a Michigan snake closely, another way to identify it is to use the *Simplified Key to Michigan Snakes* beginning on page 8. To use the key, start at the first set of paired descriptions and compare the two sets of characteristics given. Choose the one ("a" or "b") that better fits the snake and proceed to the next number indicated and compare those two. By this process of elimination, you will eventually arrive at the name of the snake and the page number of its picture, range map and description. Then read the species account and examine the map and picture to verify your identification. The illustrations on page 6 show the identifying characteristics used in the key.

This book will enable you to distinguish Michigan's 17 non-venomous snake species from one another and from the one venomous species. Equally important, this booklet introduces you to an often poorly understood but important, interesting and enjoyable part of our wildlife heritage.

When you see and positively identify one of these snakes in a natural, unconfined situation, place a checkmark or the date in the space to the left of the name of the snake. You may also want to make note of the location.

Family Colubridae
Subfamily Natricinae

❏ Kirtland's Snake – *Clonophis kirtlandii* **Page 13**

❏ Copper-bellied Water Snake – *Nerodia erythrogaster neglecta* **Page 15**

❏ Northern Water Snake – *Nerodia sipedon sipedon* **Page 17**

❏ Queen Snake – *Regina septemvittata* **Page 21**

❏ Brown Snake – *Storeria dekayi* **Page 23**

❏ Northern Red-bellied Snake – *Storeria occipitomaculata occipitomaculata* **Page 25**

❏ Eastern Garter Snake – *Thamnophis sirtalis sirtalis* **Page 27**

❏ Butler's Garter Snake – *Thamnophis butleri* **Page 31**

❏ Northern Ribbon Snake – *Thamnophis sauritus septentrionalis* **Page 33**

Subfamily Xenodontinae

❏ Northern Ring-necked Snake – *Diadophis punctatus edwardsi* **Page 35**

❏ Eastern Hog-nosed Snake – *Heterodon platirhinos* **Page 37**

Subfamily Colubrinae

❏ Blue Racer – *Coluber constrictor foxii* **Page 41**

❏ Black Rat Snake – *Elaphe obsoleta obsoleta* **Page 43**

❏ Eastern Fox Snake – *Elaphe gloydi* **Page 45**

❏ Western Fox Snake – *Elaphe vulpina* **Page 45**

❏ Eastern Milk Snake – *Lampropeltis triangulum triangulum* **Page 49**

❏ Smooth Green Snake – *Liochlorophis vernalis* **Page 51**

Family Viperidae
Subfamily Crotalinae

❏ Eastern Massasauga Rattlesnake – *Sistrurus catenatus catenatus* **Page 53**

Identifying Characteristics of Michigan Snakes

Use these illustrations with the key on page 8 to help you identify any snake found in Michigan.

Figure 1   Figure 2

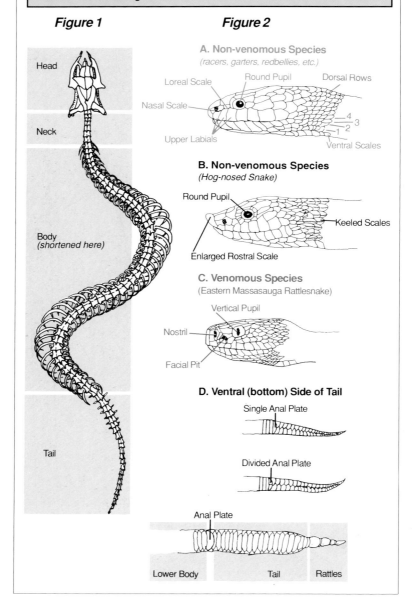

Head

Neck

Body
(shortened here)

Tail

A. Non-venomous Species
(racers, garters, redbellies, etc.)

Loreal Scale
Round Pupil
Dorsal Rows
Nasal Scale
4
3
2
1
Upper Labials
Ventral Scales

B. Non-venomous Species
(Hog-nosed Snake)

Round Pupil
Keeled Scales
Enlarged Rostral Scale

C. Venomous Species
(Eastern Massasauga Rattlesnake)

Vertical Pupil
Nostril
Facial Pit

D. Ventral (bottom) Side of Tail

Single Anal Plate

Divided Anal Plate

Anal Plate
Lower Body   Tail   Rattles

Selected Terms Used in Key and Text

Figure numbers refer to illustrations on page 6.

anal plate—scale above anal opening *(Fig. 2d)*

band—a patch of color running across the back of a snake (side to side)

blotch—an irregular patch of color

dorsal—back or top side of a snake

keel—small ridge along the center of some scales *(Fig. 2b)*

labial scales—scales bordering a snake's mouth *(Fig. 2a)*

loreal scale—scale between the eye and the nostril *(Fig. 2a)*

pit—paired heat-sensing organs on the head of a rattlesnake, between eye and nostril *(Fig. 2c)*

rostral scale—scale on the front tip of a snake's head *(Fig. 2b)*

stripe—a narrow strip of color running along the length of the back of a snake

ventral—the belly or underside of a snake *(Fig. 2a & 2d)*

A Simplified Key to Michigan Snakes

To use this key, start at the first set of paired descriptions and compare the two sets of characteristics given. Choose the one (a or b) that better fits the snake and proceed to the next number indicated and compare those two. By this process of elimination, you will eventually arrive at the name of the snake and the page number of its picture, range map and description. The illustrations on page 6 and the definitions on page 7 will help you use this key.

1. (a) A pit between eye and nostril *(fig. 2c)*; tail ending in a rattle...
      Sistrurus catenatus catenatus, Eastern Massasauga **See page 53**
   (b) No pit between eye and nostril; tail pointed **Go to number 2**

2. (a) Keels on some or all of dorsal scales of body and tail *(fig. 2b)* **Go to number 3**
   (b) Dorsal scales smooth *(fig. 2a)* **Go to number 16**

3. (a) Anal plate divided *(fig. 2d)* **Go to number 4**
   (b) Anal plate single *(fig. 2d)* **Go to number 14**

4. (a) Rostral scale turned up and keeled above *(fig. 2b)*
      Heterodon platirhinos, Eastern Hog-nosed Snake **See page 37**
   (b) Rostral scale normal *(fig. 2a)* **Go to number 5**

5. (a) No loreal, size small (12 inches or less) **Go to number 6**
   (b) Loreal present *(fig. 2a)*, adults usually larger than 12 inches **Go to number 8**

6. (a) Scale rows 17 in number *(fig. 2a)*; belly buff to light brown or pinkish **Go to number 7**
   (b) Scale rows 15; belly red....
      Storeria occipitomaculata occipitomaculata, Northern Red-bellied Snake **See page 25**

7. (a & b) Dorsal spots separate or fused to form crossbars; dark spot may or may not be present under eye...

Storeria dekayi (subspecies), Brown Snake—see text for explanation ***See page 23***

8. (a) Dorsal scales weakly keeled (keels barely visible) ***Go to number 9***

(b) Dorsal scales strongly keeled (keels easily seen) *(fig. 2b)* ***Go to number 11***

9. (a) Adult black above or with obscure blotches; juveniles spotted; 25 to 27 scale rows...

Elaphe obsoleta obsoleta, Black Rat Snake ***See page 43***

(b) Adults and juveniles yellowish to brown above with dark blotches; 23 to 25 scale rows ***Go to number 10***

10. (a) 33 to 51 dorsal blotches (average 41); anterior dorsal blotches usually 3 or 4 scales in length (Upper Peninsula)...

Elaphe vulpina, Western Fox Snake ***See page 45***

(b) 20 to 43 dorsal blotches (average 34); anterior dorsal blotches usually more than 4 scales in length (eastern Lower Peninsula)...

Elaphe gloydi, Eastern Fox Snake ***See page 45***

11. (a) Scale rows 17 to 19 in number ***Go to number 12***

(b) Scale rows 21 or more in number ***Go to number 13***

12. (a) A yellow stripe on side and 3 black lines on back; belly yellow with 4 dark stripes...

Regina septemvittata, Queen Snake ***See page 21***

(b) Back reddish brown with 4 rows of round black spots; belly reddish, with a row of black spots on either side...

Clonophis kirtlandii, Kirtland's Snake ***See page 13***

13. (a) Back uniformly black or brown, sometimes with faint dorsal blotches; belly uniformly red, orange or pink...

Nerodia erythrogaster neglecta, Copper-bellied Water Snake **See page 15**

(b) Back brown with dorsal blotches often uniting with lateral spots to form cross bands; belly mottled or with crescent-shaped spots...

Nerodia sipedon sipedon, Northern Water Snake **See page 17**

14. (a) Tail at least one-third of total length; lateral yellow stripe on scale rows 3 and 4 above the ventrals...

Thamnophis sauritus septentrionalis, Northern Ribbon Snake **See page 33**

(b) Tail length less than one-third of total length **Go to number 15**

15. (a) Upper labials normally 7; lateral yellow stripe on scale rows 2 and 3...

Thamnophis sirtalis sirtalis, Eastern Garter Snake **See page 27**

(b) Upper labials normally 6; lateral yellow stripe involves scale rows 2, 3 and 4; head about same width as neck...

Thamnophis butleri, Butler's Garter Snake **See page 31**

16. (a) Anal plate single; black-bordered brown blotches on back; top of head with a Y-shaped light spot; belly with a checkerboard pattern...

Lampropeltis triangulum triangulum, Eastern Milk Snake **See page 49**

(b) Anal plate divided **Go to number 17**

17. (a) Nasal scale single with nostril in center *(fig. 2a)*; body color uniform green....

Liochlorophis vernalis, Smooth Green Snake

(b) Two nasal scales with nostril between them *(fig. 2b)*; body not green **Go to number 18**

18. (a) A yellow ring around neck; uniformly blackish above; belly yellowish...

Diadophis punctatus edwardsi, Northern Ring-necked Snake **See page 35**

(b) No light collar; adults uniformly bluish to black above with a white chin; belly lighter blue; large size...

Coluber constrictor foxii, Blue Racer **See page 41**

Explanation of Symbols

Habitat	Temperament	Reproduction	Venom
DRY LAND	NERVOUS	LIVE-BEARING	VENOMOUS
Found in woods and meadows.	Quickly flees or threatens to strike when approached; may attempt to bite when handled.	Female snake gives birth to baby snakes.	Has glands and teeth capable of injecting a poisonous fluid (venom).
NEAR WATER	CALM	EGG LAYING	NONVENOMOUS
Found in and near wet areas—wet meadows, fens, marshes, swamps or bogs.	Cautiously moves away when approached; not likely to bite when handled.	Female snake lays eggs from which baby snakes hatch.	Not capable of injecting a poisonous fluid (venom).
WATER	VARIABLE		
Found in and along streams, rivers, lakes and ponds.	May be nervous, or calm, depending on the individual snake; usually adjusts to handling.		

KIRTLAND'S SNAKE

NEAR WATER   VARIABLE   LIVE-BEARING   NONVENOMOUS

KIRTLAND'S SNAKE
(Clonophis kirtlandii)

IDENTIFICATION:

*T*he Kirtland's Snake is a small (12 to 24 inches), reddish brown snake with black, often indistinct blotches in four rows down its back and a black head. The belly is brick-red with a row of black spots down each side. When disturbed, this snake will often flatten its body to a remarkable degree and may then remain motionless unless touched.

It may be confused with the Northern Red-bellied Snake (page 25), but the Red-bellied Snake lacks black spots along the belly and has no blotches on its back.

DISTRIBUTION:

■ Kirtland's Snake is an extremely rare species in Michigan. It has been found in a very few localities in the southern one-third of the Lower Peninsula. Most of the specimens found in Michigan have been reported from the two southernmost tiers of counties.

HABITAT AND HABITS:

■ This rarely seen snake occurs in a variety of moist habitats, which include wet meadows, tamarack swamps, open swamp-forest and vacant city lots. Earthworms and slugs are the favorite foods of Kirtland's Snake. This secretive species is believed to spend most of its time underground in the burrows of crayfish and other small animals. The tiny 5- to 6-inch young are born in late summer. There are usually 5 to 15 in a litter.

■ ***Kirtland's Snake is listed as ENDANGERED by the Michigan Department of Natural Resources (DNR) and is protected in the state. It is illegal to possess or handle this snake. Any sightings of this species should be reported to the DNR Wildlife Division, Lansing, Michigan.***

COPPER-BELLIED WATER SNAKE

NEAR WATER   VARIABLE   LIVE BEARING   N NON-VENOMOUS

COPPER-BELLIED WATER SNAKE
(Nerodia erythrogaster neglecta)

IDENTIFICATION:

*T*he Copper-bellied Water Snake is a large (30 to 56 inches) snake, uniformly colored dark brown or black. The belly is reddish, orange or yellow, and it may be shaded at the edges by the darker color of the back. Young individuals are brownish with a blotched dorsal pattern; the blotches may remain visible in some adult specimens.

The Northern Water Snake (page 17), which may occur in the same habitat, usually retains a blotched or banded pattern into adulthood and has half-moon-shaped dark spots on the belly.

DISTRIBUTION:

■ The Copper-bellied Water Snake is extremely rare in Michigan and is now found in only a few locations in the southern one-third of the Lower Peninsula. Most recent records are in Hillsdale and St. Joseph counties.

HABITAT AND HABITS:

■ Copper-bellied Water Snakes are usually found near streams, woodland ponds and river-bottom swamps. They apparently avoid fast-moving waters. Most often seen sunning on logs, banks or piles of debris at the water's edge, this species may occasionally wander away from water. They feed on amphibians (frogs, tadpoles) and small fish. The young are born in litters of 5 to 37, usually in late summer or fall.

■ *The Copper-bellied Water Snake is listed as ENDANGERED by the Michigan Department of Natural Resources (DNR) and is protected by state and federal law. It is illegal to possess or handle this snake. Any sightings of this species should be reported to the DNR Wildlife Division, in Lansing, Michigan.*

WATER   NERVOUS   LIVE-BEARING   N NONVENOMOUS

NORTHERN WATER SNAKE
(Nerodia sipedon sipedon)

IDENTIFICATION:

A medium to large (24 to 55 inches), dark-colored snake seen in or near water is likely to be this species. Most specimens have dark brown or blackish blotches or bands on a lighter brown background, but older individuals may appear uniformly black.

Unlike the rare Copper-bellied Water Snake (page 15) with its plain reddish underside, the Northern Water Snake usually has red, orange or black spots, usually half-moon-shaped, on both sides of the belly. The strongly keeled scales of these water snakes give them a dull appearance.

The young (below) are more distinctly patterned than adults, with dark bands on a light gray background.

DISTRIBUTION:

■ Northern Water Snakes occur throughout Michigan but are scarce or absent from many parts of the Upper Peninsula, particularly the western section. Some islands, such as Beaver Island in northern Lake Michigan, support large populations.

HABITAT AND HABITS:

■ This species is usually found in or near ponds, lakes, streams or rivers. They are often seen sunning alongside the water on logs, overhanging branches, rockpiles and old bridge abutments. When disturbed, they glide rapidly into the water and can swim well, both on the surface and submerged. Water snakes are harmless but are frequently misidentified as "water moccasins" and assumed to be venomous. This has led to needless persecution, and many areas that once had large populations of Northern Water Snakes now have few or none.

Water snakes are nervous and usually try to bite if cornered or restrained. If handled, they release a foul-smelling anal secretion.

Northern Water Snakes feed on frogs and fish and are frequently seen eating dead fish. They are often falsely accused of harming game fish populations, but they may actually benefit sport fishing by consuming stunted, overcrowded fish.

Female Northern Water Snakes give birth to 4 to 50 or more young in late summer or fall.

QUEEN SNAKE

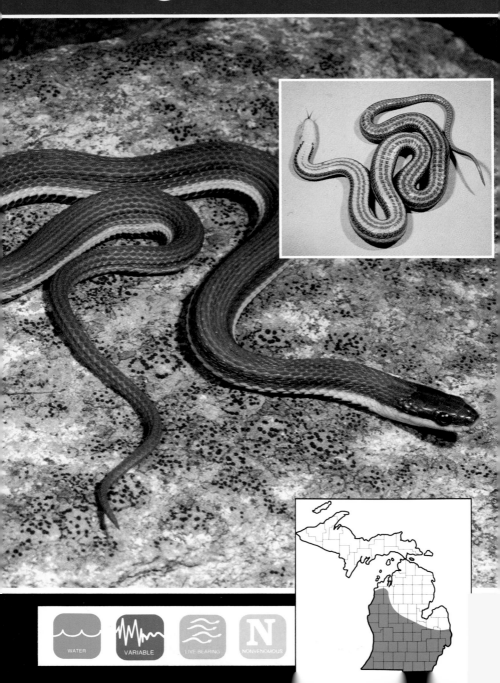

WATER VARIABLE LIVE-BEARING N NONVENOMOUS

QUEEN SNAKE
(Regina septemvittata)

IDENTIFICATION:

*T*he Queen Snake is a small to medium-sized (12 to 36 inches), slender, dark brown to gray-brown snake with a conspicuous, light yellowish stripe along each side of the body. In some specimens, three narrow, dark stripes may be visible running down the back. The belly is yellowish with four dark brown stripes; the two outer stripes are wider than the inner pair. In adults, the belly stripes may obscure the light color on the lower belly area. Queen Snakes sometimes are confused with ribbon and garter snakes (pages 27-33), but these lack the dark belly stripes and usually have a light stripe down the middle of the back. Young Queen Snakes are similar to adults but their markings are more distinct.

DISTRIBUTION:

■ The Queen Snake is uncommon to rare and occurs in scattered locations throughout the southern half of the Lower Peninsula, excluding portions of the Thumb area. An isolated population reportedly occurs on Bois Blanc Island in western Lake Huron.

HABITAT AND HABITS:

■ The Queen Snake is most often seen basking in the branches of shrubs that overhang shallow, rocky streams, but it also frequents the edges of ponds or canals. When disturbed. it drops into the water and swims to the bottom, hiding under submerged objects. The Queen Snake may bite and will release a foul-smelling musk when handled.

Queen Snakes usually eat crayfish, especially those that have recently molted and are still soft. The young are born in late summer in litters numbering from 5 to 31.

BROWN SNAKE

DRY LAND   CALM   LIVE-BEARING   NONVENOMOUS

BROWN SNAKE
(Storeria dekayi)

IDENTIFICATION:

*T*he Brown Snake is a very small (9 to 18 inches) brown or gray-brown snake, usually with two rows of parallel dark dots down the back that border a lighter middle stripe. These dots sometimes join to form bars across the back. It has a dark, downward-oriented streak on the sides of its head. The pale yellowish, brownish or pinkish belly may be edged with small black spots. The tiny young are darker than the adults and have a light band across the neck.

DISTRIBUTION:

■ Brown Snakes are found throughout the Lower Peninsula of Michigan and in the southern tip of the Upper Peninsula bordering Wisconsin. The Brown Snake population in the Lower Peninsula is intermediate between the Northern Brown Snake *(Storeria d. dekayi)* and the Midland Brown Snake *(S. d. wrightorum)*. Those in the Upper Peninsula are intergrades between the Texas Brown Snake *(S. d. texana)* and the Midland race. This mixing of subspecies may account for the variation in color pattern seen in Michigan Brown Snakes.

HABITAT AND HABITS:

■ The Brown Snake is secretive and is usually found in moist locations hiding under flat objects. They are often found in vacant city lots and disturbed areas.

Brown Snakes are most active in the spring and fall or after heavy rain showers, when they may be seen crawling across roads and sidewalks. These gentle creatures rarely bite, even when provoked. This species usually eats worms and slugs.

Females give birth to litters of 5 to 30 or more young in mid- to late summer.

DRY LAND CALM LIVE-BEARING NONVENOMOUS

NORTHERN RED-BELLIED SNAKE
(Storeria occipitomaculata occipitomaculata)

IDENTIFICATION:

*T*he Northern Red-bellied Snake is very small, usually less than 12 inches long, with a back color of brown, reddish brown or gray, sometimes with faint lengthwise stripes down the back. The belly is red, pink or orangish, without the double row of black spots seen in Kirtland's Snake (page 13).

The head is very small, and most individuals have three whitish spots behind the head that often fuse to form a light collar on the neck. This collar is less distinct than that of the Northern Ring-necked Snake (page 35). In the Upper Peninsula, this snake is commonly called the "copper-belly."

DISTRIBUTION:

■ This snake is found statewide except for the extreme southern edge of the Lower Peninsula. Although it may be rare or absent in many areas within its range, this snake can be locally abundant in some places.

HABITAT AND HABITS:

■ The Northern Red-bellied Snake can be encountered in a variety of habitats, including open woodland, meadows and abandoned farmland. It is often found under boards and debris in old dumps and trash piles.

This gentle snake is not known to bite but may curl up its "lips" when frightened or threatened. Earthworms and slugs are the favored foods. Females give birth to 1 to 20 young in mid- to late summer.

DRY LAND

VARIABLE

LIVE-BEARING

N
NONVENOMOUS

EASTERN GARTER SNAKE
(Thamnophis sirtalis sirtalis)

IDENTIFICATION:

*T*he three kinds of garter snakes in Michigan (Eastern, Butler's and Ribbon) are small to moderate-sized, with three characteristic lengthwise stripes—one on each side and one down the middle of the back. They differ in body proportions and position of the side stripes. If you count the scale rows from the large belly scales to the center of the back, you will notice that the side stripes cover different rows in each species. In the Eastern Garter Snake, this stripe is confined to scale rows 2 and 3. The stripe occurs on rows 2, 3 and 4 in Butler's Garter Snake (page 31), and on rows 3 and 4 in the Northern Ribbon Snake (page 33).

The Eastern Garter Snake is a medium-sized (18 to 54 inches) snake with an extremely variable color pattern. The background color may be black, brown or olive-green, and the three yellow, white or greenish stripes may be sharply delineated or dull and obscured.

Many individuals have dark spots between the stripes, often giving the animals a checkered appearance. Some individuals have a reddish orange coloring between the stripes. The belly is pale yellow, greenish or blue. The young are similar to the adults.

DISTRIBUTION:

■ The Eastern Garter Snake is probably the most common Michigan snake and occurs throughout the state.

HABITAT AND HABITS:

■ Woodlands, meadows, marshes, lake edges, debris piles and suburban backyards are all homes for this tolerant species. The garter snake shows a preference for damp places that support its favorite foods—earthworms, frogs, toads and small

27

fish. In urbanized areas, garter snakes seem able to live on a diet of worms.

This species varies greatly in temperament. Some specimens flatten their bodies and attempt to bite when approached, while others make no attempt to bite, even when frightened or threatened. Nearly all will smear an unpleasant anal secretion on a restraining hand. They are alert, active animals but are not as nervous as their close relative, the Northern Ribbon Snake (page 33).

Mating occurs soon after emergence from hibernation in early spring. Baby Eastern Garter Snakes are born in litters of 6 to more than 50 during midsummer.

Eastern Garter Snake swallowing a toad.

This Eastern Garter Snake is "tasting" the air with its tongue.

Butler's Garter Snake eating a worm.
(Note: The account for Butler's Garter Snake begins on page 30.)

BUTLER'S GARTER SNAKE

BUTLER'S GARTER SNAKE
(Thamnophis butleri)

IDENTIFICATION:

Butler's Garter Snake is a small (15 to 29 inches), stout-bodied, striped snake with a small, dark head. The lateral light-colored stripes on the forward part of the body are on scale row 3 and the adjacent halves of rows 2 and 4.

The background color is black, brown or olive, and the stripes are yellow and quite distinct. Some specimens display dark spots between the dorsal and side stripes.

When excited, this snake often wiggles violently back and forth with little forward movement. Compare with the Eastern Garter Snake (page 27) and the Northern Ribbon Snake (page 33).

DISTRIBUTION:

■ Butler's Garter Snake occurs in scattered populations in the eastern and south central Lower Peninsula of Michigan.

HABITAT AND HABITS:

■ This snake prefers moist meadows, marshes and the grassy edges of lakes and streams. Large populations may occur in vacant urban lots.

Butler's Garter Snake is gentle and rarely attempts to bite but will release an unpleasant musky secretion when handled. Earthworms are the favored food, but small amphibians are sometimes eaten. This species becomes tame in captivity and can live for some time on a diet of worms.

Females give birth in midsummer to litters of 4 to 20 young, which are miniatures of the adult.

NORTHERN RIBBON SNAKE

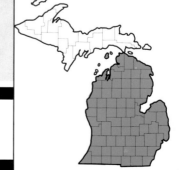

WATER

VARIABLE

LIVE BEARING

NON-VENOMOUS

NORTHERN RIBBON SNAKE
(Thamnophis sauritus septentrionalis)

IDENTIFICATION:

The Northern Ribbon Snake is 18 to 34 inches long, slender and striped, with a long tail that is about one-quarter to one-third the total length of the snake. Bright yellow or white stripes are distinct against the brown or black background color. The side stripes are on scale rows 3 and 4.

The head is long and narrow with bright, unmarked, whitish labial scales along the edge of the mouth.

Both the Eastern Garter Snake (page 27) and Butler's Garter Snake (page 31) have stouter bodies and shorter tails in relation to total length than the Northern Ribbon Snake.

DISTRIBUTION:

■ The Northern Ribbon Snake occurs throughout Michigan's Lower Peninsula.

HABITAT AND HABITS:

■ This species inhabits the grassy edges of marshes, ponds, lakes and streams. They swim well but rarely dive underwater. Ribbon snakes are alert, active animals, and when disturbed they can glide through dense vegetation with surprising speed. Frogs, tadpoles, salamanders and small fish are the favored foods. Unlike other garter snakes, ribbon snakes normally do not eat earthworms.

Ribbon Snakes rarely bite when handled but will smear a captor with a rather sweetish smelling musk. Females will give birth to 3 to 20 or more young in July or August.

DRY LAND   CALM   EGG LAYING   NONVENOMOUS

NORTHERN RING-NECKED SNAKE
(Diadophis punctatus edwardsi)

IDENTIFICATION:

*T*he Northern Ring-necked Snake is a small (10 to 20+ inches), shiny, slate-gray to bluish black snake with a yellow ring around its neck. The body scales are very smooth; the belly is plain light yellow, occasionally with a few dark spots along the midline. The young are darker than the adults but otherwise similar.

DISTRIBUTION:

■ Although the Northern Ring-necked Snake has been found throughout Michigan, it is generally rare and occurs in widely scattered and isolated populations. It can be common on some of the offshore islands in northern Lake Michigan.

HABITAT AND HABITS:

■ This species prefers moist woodlands. It is very secretive and is usually found hiding under flat objects or the bark of dead trees. Ring-necked snakes are inoffensive and rarely bite when handled. They feed on earthworms, amphibians and, occasionally, other snakes. In Michigan, they are reported to feed largely on the Red-backed Salamander *(Plethodon cinereus)*.

Female Northern Ring-necked Snakes lay from 1 to 10 elongated eggs in rotted wood or under loose bark, usually in late June. Hatching occurs in late summer.

DRY LAND   VARIABLE   EGG LAYING   N NONVENOMOUS

EASTERN HOG-NOSED SNAKE
(Heterodon platirhinos)

IDENTIFICATION:
*T*he Eastern Hog-nosed Snake is a stout-bodied snake 20 to 45 inches long, with an upturned snout. It is highly variable in color; most have dark spots and blotches on a yellowish, reddish or brown background, but some are solid black, brown or olive.

When encountered in the field, this harmless snake will often spread its neck, somewhat like a cobra, and hiss loudly. This defensive behavior has resulted in people giving this snake a number of evil-sounding nicknames, such as "puff adder" or "spreading viper."

DISTRIBUTION:
■ Although it occurs over much of Michigan's Lower Peninsula, in the Upper Peninsula the Eastern Hog-nosed Snake has been found only in Menominee County.

HABITAT AND HABITS:

■ The Hog-nosed Snake is usually found in sandy areas, especially in the open, sandy woods of the northern and western Lower Peninsula. It uses its upturned snout to dig for toads, its favorite food.

The defensive display of this snake is remarkable. When disturbed, the Hog-nosed Snake

will flatten out its neck, coil its body and its tail, and hiss loudly. It may strike out repeatedly at a threatening object, but nearly always with its mouth closed. Each strike is also accompanied by a sharp hiss.

This bluff presumably deters natural enemies such as skunks, foxes and raccoons. Many people will either flee or, unfortunately, grab a rock or stick and kill the bluffing snake, and thus miss the next part of the Hog-nosed Snake's defensive routine. If a bluffing snake is teased or grabbed, it will suddenly seem to become violently ill, appear to go into convulsions with mouth agape and tongue dragging in the dirt, and smear feces over its body. Then it will turn onto its back and lie perfectly still, appearing to be dead. Amazingly, if the "dead" snake is put "right side up" by the observer, it quickly turns on its back again, as if a dead snake must be "belly-up"! If the supposed enemy leaves, the snake soon lifts its head, tests the air with its tongue, and then crawls away as fast as possible.

Female Eastern Hog-nosed Snakes lay from 4 to more than 50 eggs underground in early summer. These hatch 60 to 70 days later into 6- to 10-inch snakes that are capable of hissing and neck-spreading before they are even free of their eggshells.

BLUE RACER

BLUE RACER
(Coluber constrictor foxii)

IDENTIFICATION:

*T*he Blue Racer is a large (4 to 6 feet), active snake with a solid bluish, greenish or gray back and a lighter, bluish belly. The head is darker than the body, and the throat and chin are white. These snakes are smooth-scaled and shiny. Newly hatched and young blue racers have a pattern of reddish brown or gray blotches and spots on a gray background (see inset photo, page 40). This pattern fades as the snakes mature and is usually gone by the time they reach 3 feet in length.

DISTRIBUTION:

■ This species occurs in the southern and western counties of Michigan's Lower Peninsula; though their numbers appear to be declining in the south, Blue Racers may be becoming more widespread in the northwestern Lower Peninsula. Records also exist for Menominee County in the Upper Peninsula.

HABITAT AND HABITS:

■ Blue Racers live in a variety of habitats, such as open woods, meadows, abandoned farmlands, raspberry thickets, and the edges of lakes and marshes.

They are alert, active snakes that gracefully glide away when approached, often climbing into low shrubs or trees to escape. When cornered, racers will coil and strike, and their tiny, sharp teeth can cause minor cuts on a human hand, but they are not venomous.

Racers eat rodents, frogs, other snakes, birds and insects. Despite the scientific name *"constrictor,"* racers do not constrict prey, but they may press larger food items against the ground with a loop of the body before and during swallowing.

Females lay from 6 to 32 eggs in rotted wood, humus or moist sand during June or July. The young snakes hatch in late summer.

BLACK RAT SNAKE

DRY LAND   NERVOUS   EGG LAYING   NONVENOMOUS

BLACK RAT SNAKE
(Elaphe obsoleta obsoleta)

IDENTIFICATION:

*T*he Black Rat Snake is very large, shiny and black with a white chin and throat. This is Michigan's largest snake, with adults frequently exceeding 6 feet in length; the record length is over 8 feet. Hatchling black rat snakes are strongly patterned with dark blotches on a light gray background. Traces of this juvenile pattern are often visible in adult specimens, though it may be reduced to a few scattered flecks of white or gray between the scales.

DISTRIBUTION:

■ In Michigan, the Black Rat Snake occurs in the southern half of the Lower Peninsula. This species is locally common in the southwestern counties, but it is rare and declining over most of its Michigan range. **This is a species of "special concern" and may not be captured or killed.**

HABITAT AND HABITS:

■ These snakes are most common in and near woodlands. They are quite arboreal and often forage and bask at considerable heights above the ground.

A species of slow and deliberate movements, Rat Snakes frequently "freeze" in position when approached, apparently hoping to escape notice. When threatened, however, they may hiss and strike and vibrate their tails nervously.

Rat Snakes feed on small mammals and birds that they catch and constrict in coils of their body; the prey animal quickly dies of suffocation or circulatory failure before being swallowed. Rat Snakes are valuable on farms because they eat rodent pests.

In June or July, females deposit from 5 to 44 eggs, usually in rotted wood or in underground burrows.

The young hatch in about 60 to 75 days.

FOX SNAKE

EASTERN FOX SNAKE
(Elaphe gloydi)
WESTERN FOX SNAKE
(Elaphe vulpina)

IDENTIFICATION:

*F*ox Snakes are fairly large (3 to 5 feet), yellowish to light brown snakes with black or dark brown blotches down the back and sides. The head of the adult may be reddish or orangish. The belly is yellowish with quadrangular black blotches.

The two forms of the fox snake in Michigan are now considered separate species (see "Distribution" below). The Eastern Fox Snake *(Elaphe gloydi)* has fewer (average 34) but larger, darker dorsal blotches than the Western Fox Snake *(Elaphe vulpina)*, which has smaller, more numerous dorsal blotches (average about 41).

DISTRIBUTION:

■ The two species of fox snake are widely separated in Michigan. The Eastern Fox Snake ranges from Saginaw Bay south along the coastal Great Lakes area to western Lake Erie. The Western Fox Snake occurs in the central and western Upper Peninsula.

HABITAT AND HABITS:

■ Flat, marshy or partially drained marsh country is the habitat of the Eastern Fox Snake. The Western Fox Snake prefers open woodlands and woodland edges, fields and dune areas. The latter is locally known (Upper Peninsula) as the "pine snake", and both subspecies are often mistakenly called "copperhead" because of the reddish head coloration (see comparison photos, page 46).

Fox snakes are normally ground-dwelling animals that eat small mammals, birds and frogs that they kill by constriction (see Black Rat Snake, page 43).

When alarmed or threatened, these harmless snakes often vibrate their tails and strike repeatedly.

The Eastern Fox Snake, in particular, is declining in numbers because of habitat destruction and pollution. Both races suffer needless persecution by humans who mistakenly believe them to be venomous.

Eastern Fox Snake-
FOUND IN MICHIGAN

Eastern Copperhead-
NOT FOUND IN MICHIGAN

Left: head of Eastern Fox Snake; right: head of Eastern Copperhead, a snake **not found in Michigan.** The Eastern Fox Snake is often called "copperhead" because of its head coloring. Note that the non-venomous fox snake has a round eye pupil, while the venomous copperhead has an elliptical eye pupil and a heat-sensing pit between eye and nostril.

Fox snakes lay from 7 to 29 eggs in June or July, which hatch in late summer. Young specimens are similar to adults but are more boldly patterned.

■ *The Eastern Fox Snake currently is listed as THREATENED by the Michigan Department of Natural Resources (DNR) and is protected in the state. It is illegal to possess or handle this snake. Any sightings of this species should be reported to the DNR Wildlife Division in Lansing, Michigan.*

Juvenile Western Fox Snake

EASTERN MILK SNAKE

DRY LAND   NERVOUS   EGG LAYING   N NONVENOMOUS

EASTERN MILK SNAKE

(Lampropeltis triangulum triangulum)

IDENTIFICATION:

*T*he Eastern Milk Snake is a slender, medium-sized (24 to 52 inches long) snake with brown or reddish brown, black-bordered blotches running down the light gray or tan back.

There is often a Y- or V-shaped light marking on the top of the neck. The belly is white with a black checkerboard pattern. Young Eastern Milk Snakes are similar to adults, but the blotches are brighter red.

DISTRIBUTION:

■ This species occurs throughout Michigan's Lower Peninsula, and there are isolated records of its occurrence in Mackinac and Marquette counties in the Upper Peninsula.

HABITAT AND HABITS:

■ These secretive snakes are found in woodlands, fields, marshes and farmlands. They often hide under boards and trash near barns and other buildings. Most often seen in spring and fall, Milk Snakes appear to be primarily nocturnal in summer. The name "Milk Snake" comes from the false belief that this species sucks milk from cows. They may indeed enter barns, or even houses, but in search of rodents. Because of this, they are also called barn or house snakes.

In addition to rodents, Eastern Milk Snakes also eat other snakes. They kill prey animals by constricting them in coils of their body. Other constrictors in Michigan are the Black Rat Snake and the Fox Snakes. Like many other harmless snakes, this species may vibrate its tail, hiss and strike when threatened. Many are unfortunately killed by persons who think they are venomous.

Female Eastern Milk Snakes lay from 6 to 24 eggs in rotted wood or under debris in early summer. In late summer or fall, the brightly colored young emerge and frequently wander into garages and basements, resulting in numerous worried phone calls to nature centers and zoos.

SMOOTH GREEN SNAKE

DRY LAND   CALM   EGG LAYING   N NONVENOMOUS

SMOOTH GREEN SNAKE
(Liochlorophis vernalis)

IDENTIFICATION:

*T*he Smooth Green Snake is a small (12 to 26 inches), bright green snake with a plain whitish or yellowish belly. Occasionally, an all-brown individual may be found, but the smooth scales and lack of spots or stripes will identify this species. The newly hatched young are dark olive or gray.

DISTRIBUTION:

■ Historically, Smooth Green Snakes have been found and recorded throughout Michigan. They remain locally common in the northern Lower Peninsula and the Upper Peninsula but are rare and found only in widely scattered locations in the southern Lower Peninsula.

HABITAT AND HABITS:

■ These snakes are usually found in open, grassy places such as meadows, pastures and marsh edges. They are active, graceful little animals that rarely attempt to bite when handled, but they will emit a musky anal secretion on a captor's hand.

Green Snakes eat insects, insect larvae and spiders and can be considered beneficial to farmers and gardeners. Their diet, however, may make them particularly vulnerable to the effects of chemical pesticides.

Females lay from 3 to 13 tiny, cylindrical eggs in burrows or under logs or rocks. Egg laying has been recorded from June into September. Considerable embryonic development may occur prior to laying; some eggs may hatch in as few as four days, but the normal incubation period is about a month.

EASTERN MASSASAUGA RATTLESNAKE

NEAR WATER

NERVOUS

LIVE-BEARING

V VENOMOUS

EASTERN MASSASAUGA RATTLESNAKE
(Sistrurus catenatus catenatus)

VENOMOUS

IDENTIFICATION:

*T*he Eastern Massasauga Rattlesnake is the only Michigan snake with a true segmented rattle on the end of its tail. Massasaugas are medium-sized (2 to 3 feet), heavy-bodied snakes with narrow necks and an elliptical (cat-like) pupil in the eye. They also have a deep facial pit on each side of the head between the eye and nostril; nerve endings in these pits can detect body heat given off by warm-blooded predators or prey.

Massasaugas are usually gray or grayish brown with dark blotches and spots down the back and sides. The belly is blackish. Young specimens are colored like the adults.

DISTRIBUTION:

■ The Eastern Massasauga occurs throughout the Lower Peninsula and on Bois Blanc Island, Mackinac County. There are no records for this or any other venomous snake in the Upper Peninsula.

HABITAT AND HABITS:

■ The Eastern Massasauga, **the only venomous species of snake in Michigan,** inhabits marshes and swamps, though they often wander into upland meadows and woods in summer. They reportedly prefer to hibernate in crayfish or rodent burrows.

These shy, secretive snakes generally retreat from a disturbance and certainly do not seek confrontations with humans. They will rattle and strike if threatened, however, and will even strike without rattling if surprised.

The venom of the Massasauga is potent, but because of their small size and short fangs, these animals are not considered to be as dangerous as their larger relatives found to the south and west of Michigan. Bites to humans are rare and fatalities rarer still, but the possibility of serious medical complications from a Massasauga bite does exist, especially for small children or persons already in poor health.

Exercise care when hiking in potential habitat, and leave alone any Massasaugas encountered. Too often, people have been bitten by rattlesnakes while attempting to handle or kill them. Any confirmed bite from this species should receive immediate attention at a hospital or other emergency medical care facility.

The Eastern Massasauga feeds largely on rodents, especially meadow mice, but they also eat frogs and other snakes. Diet is undoubtedly influenced by the availability of prey species in the habitat.

Female Massasaugas give birth to litters of 5 to 20 young in late summer. Newborn rattlesnakes have a single "button" on the tail. A new rattle segment is added at each shedding of the skin, usually several times a year, and old rattles frequently fall off. Thus the number of rattles does not correspond with the age of the snake, as is sometimes believed.

*T*he most distinguishing charac-
teristics of snakes are their lack of legs and their
long, sinuous shape. Though the shape may
appear uniform, it is composed of head, neck,
body and tail. The neck may be conspicuous or
barely distinguishable, depending on the species.
The tail begins after the anal opening or vent and
may be short, as in the Northern Water Snake, or
very long, as in the Northern Ribbon Snake.

Snakes are closely related to lizards and
evolved from lizard ancestors during the Mesozoic
Era (Age of Dinosaurs), over 100 million years
ago. Snakes have more than 200 bones, called
vertebrae, that form the backbone and, along with
the ribs, make up the entire skeleton behind the
head (except in boas, pythons and other primitive
snakes, which have tiny remnant hip and limb
bones in their bodies). This specialized skeleton
and the muscles attached to it give snakes the
shape and agility that have allowed them to
occupy many kinds of habitats throughout the
world. Many of the internal organs of snakes are
reduced in size, elongated or repositioned. For
example, most species of snakes lack a fully
developed left lung, the stomach is long and
spindle-shaped, and the kidneys are positioned
one in front of the other rather than side by side.

This elongate construction allows a
snake much freedom of motion. Snakes can move
forward in a straight line simply by moving the
wide, flat belly scales in groups, some sliding
forward, while other scales push backwards
against the ground. Snakes can also move
forward by curving their bodies and pushing with

the outside back portion of each curve. This form of movement is also used in swimming and is the way snakes move most rapidly, though they cannot move as fast as most people imagine. The top speed of the fastest Michigan snake (probably the Blue Racer) is less than 4 miles per hour, which is slower than most people can walk. Snakes have additional ways of moving, such as when climbing or moving across soft sand, but they cannot jump or arch their backs.

Another obvious feature of snakes is the forked tongue, which is a harmless sense organ and never a weapon. Snakes constantly extend and flick their tongues to detect odors. The tips of the tongue will pick up odor particles and transfer them to a special organ in the roof of the mouth (the Jacobson's or vomeronasal organ), which detects the odors and then relays the information through nerves to the brain. This enhanced sense of smell is important to snakes for detecting prey and locating mates.

A third notable characteristic of snakes is that they have no eyelids. The eyes of a snake are covered by immovable, transparent layers of skin and, although a snake can move its eyes beneath this covering, it cannot blink. Several days before a snake sheds its outer skin layer, the eye coverings appear bluish and may be so clouded that the snake has very poor vision. During such times, a snake is especially shy, secretive and nervous. After the old outer skin is shed, the eye layers are completely transparent.

The lidless eyes of snakes distinguish them from legless lizards and most other reptiles. It is the unblinking eyes of snakes that probably led to the myth that snakes can hypnotize their prey. This belief may also have arisen from the fact that snakes usually remain very still before striking, waiting for their prey to move so they can confirm its location.

The Massasauga Rattlesnake can also locate its prey and potential predators by heat detection. On both sides of the front of the head, the Massasauga has heat-detecting sense organs called pits. Each pit organ is located between and slightly below the nostril and the eye.

Snakes have no external ears or ear openings, but, contrary to popular belief, snakes are not totally deaf. Snakes can detect vibrations, especially ground vibrations, through their body and jaw bones. They can also detect low frequency airborne sounds such as those created by movement, but probably not high frequency sounds such as most birdsong.

Other interesting features of a snake's head are the jaws, teeth and saliva. Like most of the bones in a snake's head, the jaws are

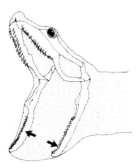

only loosely connected to each other and the adjoining bones. The lower jaw consists of two halves that are joined in the front by highly flexible connective tissue, allowing them to spread wide apart. The rear ends of the lower jaws are loosely hinged to the back of the skull, allowing the snake's mouth to open very widely. Snakes eat only other animals and cannot chew their prey, so such construction is necessary to enable a snake to swallow its prey whole, especially if the animal is larger than the snake's head.

Snakes also have several rows of small, sharply pointed, backwardly curving teeth that are attached to bones that are joined loosely to the rest of the skull. Muscles move the bones and teeth back and forth to draw prey into the mouth and down the throat of the snake. Because of their small size, the teeth of non-venomous snakes are mainly used for holding and swallowing prey.

The Massasauga Rattlesnake, however, has two elongated, hollow teeth at the front of the mouth. When the snake bites, these teeth puncture the skin of the prey and conduct venom from glands in the head into the prey.

The venom is a special form of saliva that is toxic to nerve and blood tissue. The bite of a Massasauga Rattlesnake is lethal to small animals, but in most cases it would not be lethal to animals as large as a human being. Nonetheless, the bite can be dangerous because of the damage the venom can do to tissue in the vicinity of the bite, and because it may cause shock or other reactions.

Though the bite of a venomous snake such as the Massasauga can be dangerous, the bite of a non-venomous snake is usually nothing more than shallow scratches on the skin. Such bites should be promptly washed and treated with an antiseptic to prevent infection. As with any other puncture wound, you may consider seeking medical attention. Many non-venomous snakes do not attempt to bite to defend themselves but instead release a foul-smelling fluid from their anal vent or deposit body wastes on any animal attempting to pick them up. The unpleasant smell of these fluids sometimes causes the offending animal to drop the snake. No snake stings with its tail, but many snakes will vibrate their tails as a warning. Rattlesnakes make the most obvious use of this method because the dry, hardened beads of skin on the end of the tail rattle together when shaken.

It is ironic that snakes have the false reputation of being cold and slimy. The only time a snake's skin is slimy is when it is smeared with body wastes or the foul-smelling fluid meant to repel animals attempting to catch it. The snake's skin, although covered with scales, is not covered by mucous like the scaly skin of a fish. The scales on a snake's skin are dry and the skin may feel velvety or leathery. In fact, snake skin is sometimes used in hatbands, belts, and even boots and shoes. This unfortunate practice should be discouraged, however, because it reduces desirable snake populations.

The skin of a snake may feel warm or cool or anywhere in between, depending on where the snake has been. Like all reptiles, snakes are ectothermic ("cold-blooded") and cannot produce heat internally as do mammals and birds. A snake's body temperature is often nearly the same as that of the environment. Thus, a snake that has been sunning itself may feel warm when handled by a human, whereas a snake that has been swimming or lying in the shade may feel cool.

Snakes attempt to adjust their body temperature by finding a comfortable place in their habitat. A snake may sun itself to raise its body temperature so that it may better digest food or to help it become more active. Conversely, a snake may seek shade to prevent its body from overheating on a hot day. When a snake is cool or cold, it is especially vulnerable to being caught or killed by other animals.

Because snakes would freeze in the wintertime, they must hibernate during Michigan winters. Their hibernating places, called hibernacula, are usually underground spaces below the level of freezing soil. A suitable hibernaculum—perhaps a rodent burrow, anthill or old building foundation—may be occupied by a single snake or sometimes many snakes of the same or different species. Snakes usually come out of hibernation in April or early May in Michigan and can sometimes be seen sunning themselves around the entrance to the underground cavity.

One of the first activities that snakes engage in after coming out of hibernation is mating. As the weather warms and snakes become more active, some male snakes, such as Blue Racers and Black Rat Snakes, attempt to dominate one another or chase away rivals by displays of aggression that include facing each other, raising the head and forepart of the body off the ground and pushing against one another. Female snakes release special chemicals, called pheromones, that tell the males that they are ready for mating and help the males to locate them. Mating snakes usually lie side by side or their bodies may be loosely entwined. In garter snakes, especially, several males may simultaneously try to court a single female, sometimes forming a loose "ball" of writhing snakes.

It has recently been shown that in a few snake species, including some garter and rattlesnakes, captive females may occasionally give birth to living young without having previously mated. To date, all of the offspring from unmated females appear to be males. It is not yet clear how often this phenomenon occurs in nature.

After mating, snakes usually spread out through the environment, seeking shelter and places where they can hide, rest, hunt and feed. During this time, they shed the old skin from the previous year. Hormone changes cause secretions in the skin to loosen the outer (epidermal) layer. The snake may rub its head and mouth against a rock, log or other object to begin the shedding process. The snake can then slowly crawl out of the skin, leaving behind the old skin, inside-out. The skin may be shed several more times throughout the summer. Rattlesnakes add a new segment to their rattles each time they shed.

Egg-laying snakes will lay eggs during the late spring and early summer, while snakes that give birth will continue to carry their developing young. The egg-laying species will usually deposit their eggs in a shallow burrow or

Hog-nosed Snake young emerging from their eggs in late summer.

beneath a rock or log that is warmed by the sun or in rotting vegetation where the eggs will be warmed by decomposition. The eggs hatch or the young are born during the late summer. The young soon leave the nest, or their mother, and spread out through the habitat. With the coming of fall and cold weather, all snakes begin to seek underground hibernacula and often return to the same one they used the previous year.

*F*ew people would name snakes among their favorite animals, and many people fear or at least mistrust snakes. This attitude is unfortunate because all snake species are beneficial and most are non-venomous and harmless to humans. In fact, all the snake species in Michigan will avoid contact with humans, yet many people falsely believe that snakes will chase and attack humans or attack unprovoked from ambush. Snakes are also used as a symbol of evil, and often-repeated folklore has described impossible physical abilities of snakes, such as milking cows, hypnotizing birds, rolling in loops and stinging with their tongues or tails. People usually learn a fear of snakes in early childhood from their parents or siblings. Later in life, sensationalized print and TV stories and other fearful people reinforce this fear.

Snakes should be respected but not feared. Snakes naturally fear humans but also have instincts for self-defense, as do all wild animals. It is always best to observe and enjoy snakes in their habitats without disturbing them. Never handle a snake or any wild animal unless you know how to handle it and are prepared to accept the consequences if the animal defends itself. Never allow children to handle snakes without the assistance of a knowledgeable adult. By teaching children due caution and a respect for wild creatures, you will protect them from acquiring needless fears and protect the animals from possible injury or death.

Many snakes perform a beneficial service to humans by consuming destructive animals such as insects and rodents. All have an important place in our environment. Obviously, venomous snakes can potentially harm humans, but they need be of little concern to reasonably cautious people who understand their habits and leave them alone. There is no justification for hunting and destroying snakes of any kind in their natural habitats.

In Michigan, our only venomous snake species, the Eastern Massasauga Rattlesnake, occurs in low numbers in certain marshes, swamps and nearby uplands, and is

rarely encountered by people. Further, it is a shy snake that prefers to avoid human contact. Massasaugas ocasionally wander into yards and residential areas, where their presence may be undesired—ironically, this most often occurs when recent development has usurped or disturbed their natural habitats or migration routes.

This girl is holding a Western Fox Snake, which was released after brief observation. Children should be taught to respect, not fear, snakes. Proper training in snake identification and safe handling methods is essential before attempting to pick up any snake.

SNAKES AND CONSERVATION

*L*ike many other wild animals, many kinds of snakes have declined in number because of habitat destruction and unregulated capturing and killing. Two harmless, beneficial and beautifully colored snakes, the Blue Racer and the brown and reddish yellow Eastern Fox Snake, have been nearly exterminated in southeastern Michigan. The Eastern Fox Snake is officially listed as a threatened species in Michigan. Like most other wild animals, snakes can be maintained in the environment simply by protecting or creating the habitat they require and by regulating or (when necessary) prohibiting their capture, exploitation and killing by people.

Snakes are rarely found in dense forests but prefer the edges of woods, fields and bodies of water. Dense vegetation on and near these edges will benefit snakes by providing shelter and by attracting the kinds of animals that snakes eat. Shelter includes dead trees, rotting logs, brush piles and piles of other materials such as rock, bark, wood chips, sawdust, etc. Tall grass growing between thickets of shrubs provides habitat for snakes and a great variety of other kinds of wildlife. Snakes also make use of artificial structures, just as other animals do. Pieces of plywood or sheet metal placed on the ground provide resting and hiding places for snakes.

Snakes also require a place to hibernate, called a hibernaculum. Abandoned mammal burrows, tree root systems, and other natural cavities are the usual hibernation sites, but human-made structures are also used— snakes often enter basements and crawl spaces beneath buildings if cracks or openings are present. A snake hibernaculum can be created by filling an old building foundation, well pit, or any similar hole or depression with logs, large pieces of fieldstone, broken pieces of concrete or building blocks, and then covering the filled space with a mound of loose soil. A slanting section of ribbed plastic drain pipe extending from the bottom of the pit or excavation to the surface can allow easier snake access. Scattering additional logs and other cover objects in the vicinity of the mound will increase its attractiveness for snakes and their prey. Small mammals will soon be attracted to such easily excavated sites, and snakes may soon follow. The best locations are on well drained, south-facing slopes.

Snakes can best be protected simply by leaving them alone, whether on your own or other private property or on public lands, and by urging others to do the same. Do not allow children to capture and hold snakes captive unless they are well supervised and well educated in snake identification, capture and care. Many snakes are inadvertently killed when improperly captured and held captive. Remember, it is illegal to capture, keep or kill reptiles that are

Black Rat Snake eating a mouse. Many snakes have habits beneficial to human interests, and all Michigan snakes play important roles in our state's natural ecology.

listed as "special concern," "threatened" or "endangered" species by the Department of Natural Resources. In Michigan, shooting snakes is prohibited, and the number of snakes that can be taken from the wild is limited. For further information on laws protecting snakes, contact the Michigan Department of Natural Resources.

CONTROLLING PROBLEMS CAUSED BY SNAKES

Most encounters with snakes involve harmless species that may be beneficial. If you have harmless snakes in your yard or outbuildings, realize that they are harmless and beneficial, and learn to ignore, tolerate or even enjoy them. An inability to identify snakes is no excuse for universal control; Michigan's one species of venomous snake is easily recognized (see Eastern Massasauga Rattlesnake, page 53). The Eastern Massasauga Rattlesnake usually lives in and close by the edges of marshy or swampy areas. It is a shy animal that avoids encounters with humans. If it is impossible to learn to enjoy or at least ignore non-venomous snakes in your yard, it may be necessary to reduce the chance of their presence.

To reduce the possibility of snakes being attracted to your yard, eliminate any materials that would harbor snakes or their prey, such as loose trash, wood, cardboard, paper, junk, and piles of lumber, firewood, bricks, pipe, sand, gravel, stones, bark, topsoil, leaves and compost. Garbage cans should be metal or very heavy plastic with secure, tight-fitting lids and undamaged tops, bottoms and sides. Any materials that would provide food for rodents or insects—such as pet food, wild bird seed, vegetables, fruit, etc.—should be stored in heavy plastic or metal containers with tight-fitting lids.

Keep all grass mowed as short as possible, and trim and prune the lower branches of all trees and shrubs so that no foliage comes in contact with the ground. Eliminate multiple-stemmed shrubs or confine the shrubs to three or fewer stems. Eliminate all flowers that grow in dense clumps or continuous beds, and plant or thin all other flowers so that the foliage of one flower does not touch the foliage of another. Where rats and mice are present, use traps or commonly available commercial rodenticides to reduce these populations. (Some snakes would help reduce the number of rodents.) Following these recommendations will make your yard less attractive to snakes, though snakes might still occasionally venture into the yard.

Snakes occasionally enter houses and other buildings in search of prey or in an attempt to find shelter from predators, heat or cold. They may also enter a building in the fall in search of a place to hibernate. In Michigan, Milk Snakes, Eastern Garter Snakes and Brown Snakes are the most frequent "visitors," but other species may occur as well.

To eliminate snakes from homes, follow these four recommendations:

1 Non-venomous snakes are most easily caught by hand. (NEVER attempt to handle a snake unless you are certain it is non-venomous!) Simply catch any non-venomous snake found in the home and release it away from the house. Because non-venomous snakes have tiny teeth and may bite in self-defense, wear a pair of gloves and long sleeves to protect the skin from an attempted bite. If the snake hides before it can be caught, place several damp cloths on the floor and cover them with a dry cloth. Snakes will often crawl between the cloths, where they can then be caught.

The Eastern Massasauga Rattlesnake rarely enters homes or buildings, but if a snake in the home is positively identified as a Massasauga, it is best to seek professional advice or assistance before trying to move it.

2 Snakes usually enter the home through openings at or near the ground line. Keep them out by inspecting and repairing the foundation at the ground line, the place where the foundation meets the frame of the house (the sill plate), and around any windows and doors at ground level. Touch up the foundation with masonry wherever you see gaps, holes or cavities on the inside and above ground on the outside. Close all openings that are 1/4 inch wide or wider with any convenient material—insulation, steel wool, caulk, wood or masonry. If rodents are also a problem, these openings must be tightly sealed with sheet metal, hardware cloth or masonry. Keep in mind that most snakes do not dig holes but do take advantage of any existing opening that is large enough for them to enter.

3 Clean up all materials that provide food and cover for slugs, earthworms and rodents to reduce the snakes' food supply. Store all foods and anything edible (such as pet and bird food) in tight-fitting containers. Clean up all spilled food, grease, etc. Remove accumulations of wood, cloth, paper, cardboard, etc.

4 If rodents are present, you can use traps or the readily available commercial rodenticides as directed on the labels. It is important to note, however, that the presence of rodents and the use of poisons to eliminate them pose a greater hazard to the occupants of a house than the presence of non-venomous snakes. Further, the elimination of rodents is no guarantee that an occasional snake will not enter the house.

PREVENTING AND TREATING SNAKEBITES

Most snakebites to humans occur when people try to tease, handle or, unfortunately, kill snakes. Few, if any, Michigan snakes will attack without being threatened in some way, and the best way to prevent snakebite is to simply leave snakes alone and unmolested. When snakebite does occur, it is important to identify the snake species involved—the great majority of bites will be from non-venomous snakes. Treating a bite from a non-venomous snake as though it were venomous will subject the victim to needless worry and expose him/her to possible complications from unneeded medical treatments.

Bites from non-venomous snakes are usually no more serious than scratches. Cleanse the wound with soap and water, treat with any commonly available antiseptic, and consider seeking professional medical advice as you would with any puncture wound. If you are uncertain whether the bite came from a venomous or a non-venomous snake, seek professional medical advice. A bite from a venomous snake will usually produce some swelling, reddening of the skin, dizziness and nausea within minutes after the bite, if venom is injected. (Note that

The tiny Northern Brown Snake is often found near human dwellings in suburban and rural areas.

venomous snakes do not always inject venom when they bite.)

In any case of venomous snakebite, the best advice is to get professional medical attention as fast as possible, with the least amount of physical movement by the bite victim. Do not attempt to treat a bite from a venomous snake "in the field" unless you have had specific medical training for this problem. Improper treatment could cause greater injury than the bite itself or could intensify the effect of the venom. Remember, overexcitement and exercise, such as running, can cause the venom to spread more quickly through the body. A bite from Michigan's native Massasauga Rattlesnake, while potentially serious, is almost never fatal, and most victims will experience a complete recovery. (Note: Because of the rarity of venomous snakebite in Michigan, some emergency room physicians in the state may be unfamiliar with treatment procedures; information should be readily available from poison control centers in the major cities, however.)

ECOLOGY OF MICHIGAN SNAKES

Aquatic fish and frog eaters

Copper-bellied Water Snake

Northern Water Snake

Aquatic crayfish eater

Queen Snake

Marsh-dwelling, venomous, frog and rodent eater

Eastern Massasauga

Near shore and upland foragers

Eastern Garter Snake *(opportunistic feeder)*

Northern Ribbon Snake *(mainly eats small frogs)*

Terrestrial, secretive worm eaters

Brown Snake

Butler's Garter Snake

Kirtland's Snake

Northern Red-bellied Snake

Northern Ring-necked Snake *(also eats salamanders)*

Sandy-soil-dwelling toad eater

Eastern Hog-nosed Snake

Terrestrial, meadow-dwelling insect eater

Smooth Green Snake

Terrestrial, rodent-eating constrictors

Black Rat Snake

Eastern Fox Snake

Eastern Milk Snake

Western Fox Snake

Terrestrial, frog- and rodent-eating racer

Blue Racer

FOR MORE INFORMATION

Behler, J.L., and F.W. King. 1979. *The Audubon Society Field Guide to North American Reptiles and Amphibians.* New York: Alfred A. Knopf, Inc.

Conant, R., and J.T Collins. 1991. *A Field Guide to Reptiles and Amphibians of Eastern and Central North America* (3rd ed.). Boston: Houghton Mifflin Co.

Ernst, C.H., and R.W. Barbour. 1989. *Snakes of Eastern North America.* Fairfax, Va.: George Mason University Press.

Ernst, C.H., and G.R. Zug. 1996. *Snakes in Question.* Washington, D.C.: Smithsonian Institution Press.

Greene, H.W. 1997. Snakes: *The Evolution of Mystery in Nature.* Berkeley and Los Angeles: University of California Press.

Halliday, T.R., and K. Adler (eds.). 1986. *The Encyclopedia of Reptiles and Amphibians.* New York: Facts On File, Inc.

Harding, J.H. 1997. *Amphibians and Reptiles of the Great Lakes Region.* Ann Arbor, Mich.: University of Michigan Press.